E

*Eat Like a Local- Sarasota: Sarasota Florida Food Guide*

I have lived in the Sarasota area since 1998 and learned about many great places that I want to try. –Conoal

*Eat Like a Local: Connecticut: Connecticut Food Guide*

This a great guide to try different places in Connecticut to eat. Can't wait to try them all! The author is awesome to explore and try all these different foods/drinks. There are places I didn't know they existed until I got this book and I am a CT resident myself! –Caroline J. H.

*Eat Like a Local: Las Vegas: Las Vegas Nevada Food Guide*

Perfect food guide for any tourist traveling to Vegas or any local looking to go outside their comfort zone! – TheBondes

*Eat Like a Local-Jacksonville: Jacksonville Florida Food Guide*

Loved the recommendations. Great book from someone who knows their way around Jacksonville. –Anonymous

*Eat Like a Local- Costa Brava: Costa Brava Spain Food Guide*

The book was very well written. Visited a few of the restaurants in the book, they were great! Sylvia V.

*Eat Like a Local-Sacramento: Sacramento California Food Guide*

As a native of Sacramento, Emerald's book touches on some of our areas premier spots for food and fun. She skims the surface of what Sacramento has to offer recommending locations in historical, popular areas where even more jewels can be found. –Katherine G.

# EAT LIKE A LOCAL- AUCKLAND

*Auckland New Zealand Food Guide*

**Artem Axenov**

CZYK Publishing Since 2011.
CZYKPublishing.com
Eat Like a Local

Mill Hall, PA
All rights reserved.
**ISBN:** 9798359087629

# BOOK DESCRIPTION

Are you excited about planning your next trip? Do you want an edible experience? Would you like some culinary guidance from a local? If you answered yes to any of these questions, then this Eat Like a Local book is for you. Eat Like a Local - Auckland by Artem Axenov offers the inside scoop on food in Auckland. Culinary tourism is an important aspect of any travel experience. Food has the ability to tell you a story of a destination, its landscapes, and culture on a single plate. Most food guides tell you how to eat like a tourist. Although there is nothing wrong with that, as part of the Eat Like a Local series, this book will give you a food guide from someone who has lived at your next culinary destination.

In these pages, you will discover advice on having a unique edible experience. This book will not tell you exact addresses or hours but instead will give you excitement and knowledge of food and drinks from a local that you may not find in other travel food guides.

Eat like a local. Slow down, stay in one place, and get to know the food, people, and culture. By the time you finish this book, you will be eager and prepared to travel to your next culinary destination.

# OUR STORY

Traveling has always been a passion of the creator of the Eat Like a Local book series. During Lisa's travels in Malta, instead of tasting what the city offered, she ate at a large fast-food chain. However, she realized that her traveling experience would have been more fulfilling if she had experienced the best of local cuisines. Most would agree that food is one of the most important aspects of a culture. Through her travels, Lisa learned how much locals had to share with tourists, especially about food. Lisa created the Eat Like a Local book series to help connect people with locals which she discovered is a topic that locals are very passionate about sharing. So please join me and: Eat, drink, and explore like a local.

# TABLE OF CONTENTS

# DEDICATION

This book is dedicated to Doris, my partner in crime when it comes to tackling all that Auckland has to offer when it comes to food. And to Jack, my partner, my rock, the person who keeps me grounded in this little thing we call life.

# ABOUT THE AUTHOR

Artem is a late 20-something who grew up in Wellington before making the move to Auckland to pursue his marketing career. Food was one of the saving graces of this sprawling metropolis, and Artem explored everything it had to offer. Food is the best way to experience Auckland. Food is the best way to experience New Zealand. Food is life. Food is love.

# HOW TO USE THIS BOOK

The goal of this book is to help culinary travelers either dream or experience different edible experiences by providing opinions from a local. The author has made suggestions based on their own knowledge. Please do your own research before traveling to the area in case the suggested locations are unavailable.

**Travel Advisories**: As a first step in planning any trip abroad, check the Travel Advisories for your intended destination.
https://travel.state.gov/content/travel/en/ traveladvisories/traveladvisories.html

# FROM THE PUBLISHER

Traveling can be one of the most important parts of a person's life. The anticipation and memories that you have are some of the best. As a publisher of the *Eat Like a Local*, Greater Than a Tourist, as well as the popular *50 Things to Know* book series, we strive to help you learn about new places, spark your imagination, and inspire you. Wherever you are and whatever you do I wish you safe, fun, and inspiring travel.

Lisa Rusczyk Ed. D.
CZYK Publishing

*"First we eat, then we do*
*everything else."*

M.F.K. Fisher

Auckland Food. Where to start? You've likely landed in the city of sails because it's where most international flights land. For some, this city will be a blip on the circuit track that is New Zealand. For others who dare to delve into the heart of Auckland, it may become a fond memory of a city just big enough to give you everything you want, and yet just small enough to not be a pain in the ass. Auckland is not a perfect city by any means. But on the trifecta of things to do, places to eat at, and areas to explore, it comes pretty damn close.

Come, and explore this wonderful city, the city of sails.

**Auckland**
New Zealand

# Auckland
# New Zealand
# Climate

| | High | Low |
|---|---|---|
| January | 75 | 61 |
| February | 76 | 61 |
| March | 73 | 59 |
| April | 68 | 55 |
| May | 64 | 51 |
| June | 60 | 47 |
| July | 58 | 45 |
| August | 59 | 46 |
| September | 62 | 49 |
| October | 64 | 52 |
| November | 67 | 54 |
| December | 72 | 59 |

## GreaterThanaTourist.com

Temperatures are in Fahrenheit degrees.
Source: NOAA

# 1. INTRODUCTION TO AUCKLAND

Auckland is New Zealand's biggest city. To give you an idea, it has a population of 1.65 million and this represents a third of the population of New Zealand. Something you need to understand is that Auckland is actually four cities that grew into each other and were eventually unified under one mega council.

New Zealander's penchant for single-story houses means the city is very spread out. From one end to the other, it will take you close to two hours to traverse. That's without traffic. Fortunately for us, huge numbers of the best cafes and restaurants are located within a 5-6km radius of the city centre. This makes exploring the foodie scene a lot easier and cuts down on time spent on public transport. In fact, you can usually walk between most locations.

Auckland is a harbour city, and known as the city of sails. Although surprisingly it doesn't have the largest marina, that title goes to Picton, a small town on the South Island. Once you pass the harbour bridge from the city, you get to the North Shore. It can be a pain to reach during rush hour, so best to avoid crossing the bridge in the mornings and evenings.

If you're sick of the city, just an hour's drive will get you right into the thick of nature. There are heaps of places to head to, whether it's Piha with the black sand beach or the Hunua Waterfalls. There are boundless options of where to drive and enjoy the best of nature. Going slightly farther afield Tauranga, Rotorua, and Kerikeri are all around 2.5-3 hours drive. This means there are a lot of day trips or overnight options!

Anyway, welcome to Auckland! Enjoy the city. Make the most of our foodie scene. Get out into nature and see what this beautiful country has to offer.

# 2. TO CASH OR NOT TO CASH?

You probably don't know this, but New Zealand was a testing territory for the Eftpos system. This was a debit card system that pre-dated chip cards. While we fell a bit behind in implementing pay wave, we've mostly caught up and most places will let you tap and pay. At the rest, you can still pay with your chip card just by inserting it.

Very few places won't accept cards. The most common would be a local corner store (known as a dairy colloquially) or some dollar stores. But even these will just have a minimum spend to use your card. In short, if you feel better about having cash very few places will turn you away. If you'd rather just use your card then you won't have any issues either.

For getting around using public transport, buy a hop card as soon as you can. You load money onto the card and then get discounted rates on public transport. It also lets you load up a day pass for unlimited travel around the city. Combined with the app, you'll easily plan and pay for trips. Also make sure to download the AT Parking app as this makes it super easy to pay for parking across the city.

# 3. TIPPING CULTURE

The short answer here is there is no need to. New Zealand has very strong labour laws and a fair minimum wage that has recently been raised. The staff will certainly appreciate any gratuities, but don't feel obligated to tip. You'll never have anyone ask you for a tip, except a few places where it's been baked into their POS. There is no reduction of service, and no improvement either if you do tip. Everyone ends up being treated the same whether you tip or don't.

Tip jars at cafes are fairly common, but you'll notice they're never full and I can't really remember seeing anyone ever use these. Half the time it's labelled as 'buy the staff a round of drinks' more so than 'tips'. Some cafes do have hanging coffees – you can pay it forward by buying a coffee or a meal for someone in need.

Outside of hospitality tips again aren't expected nor required. I think you'd confuse most people if you tried to tip them for doing their job.

# 4. GETTING AROUND AUCKLAND

Getting around can be a bit tricky if you rely on public transport. Areas don't tend to be well connected, however, it can be done with the right planning. AT transport is the governing body for all transport in Auckland, and you can quickly find the best public transport route. An AT Hop card is the best way to pay for your fares.

You will find scooters littered throughout the inner city to make short trips quick and easy. There are a few different companies, so you may need a few apps to get full coverage. Uber or Ola is an inexpensive way to get around, most trips in the inner city should come to no more than $10-$15.

At the end of the day, the car is king in Auckland. It's the easiest and fastest way to get around. And the traffic really isn't as bad as everyone says. Just avoid the highways in the morning and between 5-7pm. Parking is not a big issue everywhere apart from the CBD. Fortunately, there is a huge parking building called the Victoria St Carpark. It's the simplest way to find a park in the city, and after 6pm it's only $4 for the entire evening.

# 5. WE START WHERE WE LAND

The first stop on your food journey is at the airport. Specifically the domestic terminal. Best Ugly Bagels is an Auckland institution that is slowly spreading to permeate the rest of the country. There are a half dozen locations nationwide, but the closest when you land is at the Domestic Terminal of Auckland Airport.

The Domestic Terminal is just a short 10-minute walk away, and it is well worth it to pick up a delicious bagel. The Yoda is a bit of a cult classic. But to be honest, you can't go wrong. I always love to pick up a PB&J when I'm catching a 7am flight. And if I'm ever in the area during lunch, I love to go for a Tuna Melt.

Best Ugly also sells almost all their ingredients so you can re-create their creations at home. This can make an excellent snack on the go, and their bagels last for ages if you have access to a freezer. To reheat, simply put in a toaster, usually for about 2x the maximum time if reheating from frozen.

# 6. TAKE A TRIP TO PARIS, OR ROMA?

You've arrived in the city. Now what? Of course, you are hungry. And after a long-haul flight with what can maybe pass as food, you want the best. Head along to Amano. A gastronomical feast awaits you. It's located just a block away from Queen Street, right in the heart of Auckland.

For small eats, make a bee-line for the bakery. Pick up a pastry, a sandwich, and a coffee. Basically, everything here is delicious so don't feel shy. The donuts are a particular favourite of mine, with their ever-changing seasonal selections. Amano also does an excellent chocolate croissant that is flaky and perfectly buttery.

For bigger bites, have a sit-down meal and enjoy tasty Italian cuisine. Sip on a glass, or bottle, of vino. Relax and unwind and enjoy la dolce vita, down here at the end of the earth. You've made it. You're here. Enjoy the food!

# 7. LA DOLCE VINO?

After stuffing yourself with a fantastic Italian lunch, you'll probably want a few hours' rest. Why not make it on a boat? And on your way to an Island? And an Island that is known for its wine? Need I say more?

That's right, just a few minutes' walk from Amano is the pier to the ferry which will take you to Waiheke Island. Enjoy the 40-minute ferry, and grab a few Pals while you're on board. NZ is well known for its drinking culture, so never feel shy to order a cheeky drink, or five.

Pals is the RTD du jour right now. Available in a huge range of flavours, and always increasing. The simple design and fresh flavours have propelled this to the forefront of the RTD culture in New Zealand. The watermelon mint and the peach passionfruit are two of the best flavours you can find.

# 8. WAIHEKE WINE AWAITS

Waiheke Island can be overwhelming to the uninitiated. But the great news is that you cannot go wrong. The wineries range from low to high end, the taxis operate till midnight, and the food is top-notch. Best of all the scenery will leave you coming back for more.

Located a short 40min ferry ride from Auckland, Waiheke is a popular escape for locals. It's far enough to feel out of the city but close enough to make a one-day trip. The entire island is littered with vineyards, and almost all of these have an attached restaurant and cellar door. You can take a wine tour or organise one yourself. For a first run, I'd recommend a wine tour, it'll also absolve you of finding a sober driver.

Some of my favourite vineyards are Batch, Peacock Sky Vineyard, and Stonyridge. With over 30 wineries you'd need several days to try each one. Alternatively, head to the local wine shop that stocks wines from every winery on the island.

# 9. BACK, BACK, BACK IN AUCKLAND AGAIN

Now that you've had your fill of Waiheke vino, it's time to relax and unwind. Head over to Fed Deli right opposite the Sky Tower. This American-inspired diner serves up some of the best comfort food in the city. Their cheesecake platter and poutine are a must-try.

Don't forget to order a bottomless coffee, this will serve as a great introduction to NZ coffee. There will be many more cafes to try on your journey, but this is a nice place to begin. You can get it as a cold brew, or filter. And for the noncaffeinated, there is a bottomless tea option.

After you've finished off your poutine and cheesecake, the city is your oyster to explore. You could head to the Sky Casino to try your luck, check out a risqué show at Men of Steel, catch some theatre at the civic, or boogie the night away at one of the many clubs in the city. Whatever your vice, the city has you covered.

# 10. PASTRIES ON K'ROAD

If you're ever up nice and early, make a beeline for Fort Greene on Karangahape Road (K'Road). Here you'll find some of the best croissants, breads, and pastries in the city. Fort Greene uses only season produce, so the menu changes often. They make as much as possible in-house, and the rest is sourced from local producers.

The chocolate almond croissant my absolute favourite, and it often sells out within a few hours. There have been many disappointed mornings of driving to Fort Greene only to find out I was too late! It's the perfect mix of crunchy, and soft that will leave you wanting more. The chocolate mixes with the almond and creates an ideal flavour combination. If you've ever had one before you will know what this is all about. And if you haven't then you are in for a real treat.

Alongside the baked goods, you'll find a range of breakfast foods and delicious sandwiches. The Kimchi Cheese Toasty makes for a hearty meal, especially when combined with one of their pastries. They're not known for their coffee, but it is up to standard. Although personally I prefer to get a cup from Daily Daily Coffeemakers just a short 2 minute walk away.

# 11. THE PIE PIPER & DOORNUTS

Just down a few doors from Fort Greene, you'll find The Pie Piper & Doornuts. This tiny store specialises in American-style desserts. Come here for their donuts, cakes, and pies. The flavours are authentic and out of this world. They use quality ingredients and make everything from scratch.

The boston cream doornut is a personal favourite, their custard is the perfect complement to the dark chocolate ganache on top. There is also a range of vegan donuts, that are just as good as their regular alternatives. The Pie Piper supplies these vegan donuts to a vegan fast food chain called Lord of the Fries, so you know they're good.

If you're feeling something savoury, they serve up a range of diner-style dishes like fried chicken and hoagies. Everything can be ordered from Uber Eats if you don't feel like leaving your bed. There's nothing as indulging as having a hoagie and donut in bed before you start the day.

# 12. TRY A TIPPLE

While you're on K'road, check out one of the premier wine shops in Auckland. Everyday Wine stocks the more interesting wines made in NZ. Think orange wine, chilled reds, organic and more. Come in and chat with the workers, who are all passionate vinos. They'll help you find the perfect bottle to take on a picnic. You could even try out their reusable wine bottles if you're in Auckland for a longer stay.

# 13. PASTA, PASTA, AND MORE PASTA

My final tip for your K'road experience is to check out one of the many Italian restaurants. Cotto is a fan favourite and always impresses. Make sure to make a reservation as it tends to fill up, even early in the week. If Cotto is full, you're in luck as Coco's Cantina across the road is another excellent option for all your carb needs.

And if both of those are full, Carmen Jones right next to Coco's serves up lively Spanish fare to sate your rumbling tummy. As you can see, K'road is a thriving foodie scene and can take you from breakfast all the way through lunch and dinner.

# 14. WINE AWAY THE DAYS

There are many wine bars in Auckland, and one of the best is Beau on Parnell Road. It's a cosy little spot that's perfect to while away the evening as you sip your way through their wine list. In the back, you'll find a courtyard which has a really romantic atmosphere. No matter where you sit though, the wine and food are why you'll keep coming back.

Beau has an excellent wine list that changes on a regular basis, both by the glass and by the bottle. The staff here are incredibly knowledgeable and passionate about the wines. They'll be more than happy to suggest the right one if you give them an idea of what you enjoy. You'll be able to have a taste of a few before you take the plunge.

The food menu is not to be missed. The shoestring fries are the perfect indulging snack to go with any of the wines. Burrata is a big trend at the moment, and Beau does it particularly well. Finally, if they have the octopus, you have to get it. It's smoky, full of flavour and will redeem any bad octopus you've had in the past.

# 15. BE TAKEN CARE OF

The best place to start or end the night is at a hidden cocktail bar. The Caretaker is here to soothe your soul with your perfect cocktail. The twist at this bar is that there is no menu. The bar staff are experts in their fields and will help you nail down your perfect drink. They'll ask for your preferences, anything to avoid, and what you're looking for. After that, you'll get a custom-made cocktail, and if you're not satisfied, they'll remake it free of charge.

I've had many a night sipping my way through one excellent cocktail after another at the Caretaker. The bar is dimly lit in the best way possible and has a real speakeasy vibe. You enter by going through an unassuming door and down some stairs. Be sure to call ahead and book a table as this bar gets very busy, especially Thursdays-Saturdays. An hour-long wait can be expected later in the evening.

One tip I have is if they've nailed your cocktail and you think it's perfect, ask them to improve upon it and maybe give some ideas. My sister and I did this one time and she managed to walk away with several new favourites!

# 16. FIESTA IN COMMERCIAL BAY!

There's not a huge range of tequila at most bars in New Zealand, that was until Ghost Donkey galloped onto the scene. Located in Commercial Bay, this bar is an attack on the senses. The ceiling is covered in pink LEDs and it gets pumping over the weekend. If the name sounds familiar, it may be because of their original Las Vegas branch. That's right, this is the same Ghost Donkey you can find in Sin City.

Best of all they serve up delicious Mexican cuisine, from guacamole to tacos and quesadillas. The food here is worth coming for, and the range of tequilas and mezcal is worth staying. If you want a slightly more chill experience, then come along for lunch. Ghost Donkey is formally part of Commercial Bay's food area, and as such is open from lunchtime through to the evening.

The staff here do their best to create a fiesta vibe and match the energy of the music pumping through the speakers.

# 17. PREGO

When you're looking for a classy dinner in Auckland, Prego is the easiest choice. Located in the heart of Ponsonby, it serves authentic Italian cuisine. They're most known for the pasta and pizza, both of which are excellent. While being on the pricier side of restaurants in Auckland, it's well worth the little bit more for the quality of food you receive.

The mushroom risotto is one of my favourites, and I can never pass up a good Margherita. Simple as these may be, they're quintessential Italian: quality ingredients prepared with love. There is a menu for mains as well, and these are on the same level as the aforementioned dishes.

The wine list spoils you with a wide array of local and imported wines. You'll find some non-alcoholic spirit cocktails, not something you see at every establishment.

# 18. TRUFFLE FRIES & ITALIAN SHARING

Auckland has a lot of great Italian food. However, Farina holds a special place in my heart as it's the first Italian restaurant I discovered long before I moved to the city. It's a relatively small restaurant that gives a special cosy vibe perfect for the family-style Italian food they serve.

It's often fully booked but luckily they can usually squeeze you in at the bar. The open kitchen is right in front of the bar, which makes for a great night watching the chefs while imbibing the food and drink.

I'm a sucker for shoestring fries, and Farina does a particularly excellent job with their truffle fries. There's something delectable about ordering a white wine and truffle fries and living your best life. You can share most of the food, and they have a brick oven for perfect Italian-style pizzas.

If you happen to be in search of a place to host a party, Farina has you covered. You can decide on a per-person cost and they will bring out dishes within that budget. It's a great way to sample a wide range of their menu at a predictable price, usually in the region of $50+ per person.

# 19. ISLAND STYLE DONUT HYPE

There are few shops in Auckland that have as much hype and fanfare surrounding them as the Doe Donut Shop in Grey Lynn. Launched initially during covid as a side hustle by a couple of corporate workers, it became an overnight sensation. The star here is the special island-style donut batter which makes for a thick and fluffy donut.

What's really special is the over-the-top flavours. Everything is 100% handmade, and you can often see the behind-the-scenes process on their insta stories. With flavours like Pandan, Tiramisu, Rhubarb Crumble and more it's easy to see the appeal! The best part is the flavours revolve on a weekly basis, so there's always a reason to pop in.

A word of warning, because of the hype surrounding the store they sell out often. My best advice is to order online to ensure you get the flavours you want to try.

Doe Donuts sometimes does island-style meals that are to die for. So if you're lucky and happen to be in Auckland when they're offering this, don't hesitate to order. It's an amazing way to experience Pacific Island cuisine that is authentic and made with love.

# 20. VEGAN PASTRIES?!

Vegan options have started to slowly permeate Auckland. While you can easily find a few options in most cafes and restaurants, there are far fewer places that are 100% vegan. Tart Bakery is a standout for creating vegan baked goods and treats that are impossible to distinguish from the real deal. Don't ask me how they do it, maybe they made a deal with the devil himself.

Located in Grey Lynn town, it's worth coming not only for the bakery but for the rest of the cafes nearby. The Postal Service café in particular stands out for its hip feel and tasty treats.

For Tart Bakery itself, their donuts and croissants are a particular treat. And I can never pass up a classic Kiwi Pie, something you should definitely try at least a few times on your trip. These pies are quite different to other countries' versions. Tart does a great job at transforming them to be vegan without any recognisable change in taste.

# 21. PICNIC IN A SECRET SPOT

If you're looking to escape from the hustle and bustle of the city, the Parnell Rose Gardens is one of the best places to check out. You'd never know it's only minutes from the CBD, the area is serene and there is a lagoon to relax at or take a dip in.

Stop at a supermarket to pick up a roast chicken, some deli meats, cheeses, salads and buns for a classic kiwi dinner. There is a coin-operated BBQ right by the lagoon where you can cook up any raw meat you got earlier after strolling through the roses.

If you're looking for a bit more of a trek, you can start out in Parnell Village and follow some hidden tracks through the native bush. This is maybe a 30-minute walk from start to finish and a wonderful way to experience some nature. Drinking is permitted throughout this walking path and the lagoon area. So you can pick up some craft beers or local wine to enjoy with dinner.

# 22. HIKE UP A VOLCANO

Everyone needs some exercise every once in a while, and Mount Eden is the perfect walk to fill that craving. There are multiple ways to get to the peak, meaning it's hard to get lost. The top offers an almost 360-degree view of the city. You may or may not know, but Auckland has a number of dormant volcanoes. Many of the mountains around are all past volcanoes – Mount Eden, Mount Albert, Mount Wellington, and Mount Roskill being the most prominent.

One of the unique things about Mount Eden is the crater at the top. It'll give you an idea about its past as an active volcano. Be careful not to walk down to the bottom of the crater though. The sides are very steep and there are warnings not to head there.

Once you've taken your photos and enjoyed the views, you can head down to Mount Eden village for a coffee and a pastry. Or if you're in the mood to shop, Newmarket and its newly renovated mall aren't far away.

# 23. SEE THE CIRCUS IN MT EDEN

There are many great cafes in Mount Eden, however, Circus Circus is a bit of an institution amongst locals. A great spot to bring the kids if they're with you. This café is as you may have guessed, circus themed. Come into the big top and order some classic New Zealand café fare.

Circus Circus has been a hit ever since it opened in 1995. The space is split into two areas: the indoors, and the garden space. Sitting outside in the garden is particularly lovely during the warmer months. The food and coffee are great, my go-to is the eggs benedict, a side order of shoestring fries and an iced americano.

# 24. HEAD TO OLAFS FOR BRUNCH

Olaf in my opinion is one of the best brunch places in Auckland. It's often busy and it pays to book in advance. Their specialty is pastries and breads, which they pull off with aplomb. I'm a huge fan of their berry tarts, normally only available during Summer. The pastry is so fine and crumbles in your mouth as the pastry cream melts with the berries, YUM!

If you want to get some pastries and breads for a picnic, this is a great place to stock up. And just around the corner is Glengarrys, a wine store that has an excellent range of local and international wines.

While the bakery may be where they began, their brunch menu is no less impressive. The classic choice has to be an eggs benedict, known locally as an eggs benny. If you're ever somewhere for brunch and not sure what to get, the eggs benny is usually a solid choice.

There is a great selection of vegetarian options available like the truffled mushrooms on sourdough. Vegans can be easily catered to by omitting some ingredients like cheese or honey.

# 25. HOW MANY DUMPLINGS CAN YOU EAT?

Any Aucklander can tell you fond memories of indulging, and overeating, the dumplings on Dominion Road. There are a lot of different restaurants that serve up delicious dumplings. The most popular is Barilla, with two outlets just over 1km apart. You can nab 20 flavourful dumplings for under $20. Finishing the whole plate can be a bit of a challenge, so don't hesitate to take them away.

In addition to dumplings, every restaurant has a huge range of authentic Chinese dishes. These are mostly made for sharing, so don't let the low prices fool you into thinking the portions are small. Bring a group, order some dishes and have a swell time. Many of the restaurants offer BYO as well, making them a perfect spot for cheap eats.

Dominion Road itself is a mecca for every Asian cuisine imaginable, and you'll often find the best of the best at these little shops. The prices are low, the food is delicious, and you'll want to keep coming back for more.

# 26. XI'AN NOODLES = LIP SMACKING GOOD

There are many famous restaurants and takeout shops in Auckland. But few have risen to the cult status of Xi'an Food Bar. With 7 locations across the city and one in Hamilton, it's clear that Aucklanders are loving what Xi'an Food Bar is doing. As the name suggests, these all serve up dishes from the Xi'an province in China.

The most popular dish is hand-pulled noodles with Xi'an-style stewed pork. Ask for an extra-large size, trust me it's worth the extra $1. Make sure to mix everything together and then slurp your way to heaven. The stewed pork and sauce cover the hand-pulled noodles to create a flavour sensation. It's a little greasy, in the best way possible. The regular version is on the spicy side, so ask for no chilli if you're not great with spicy food like me.

Another favourite of mine is the Chinese pork burger. The pulled pork with sauce is next level of juicy and flavourful. A hack I came up with is to get the hand-pulled noodles and the Chinese burger, then add the meat from the burger to the noodles for an extra serving of meat. This should easily feed two people for a medium sized meal.

# 27. MARMAGEDDON!

It was an unassuming day in 2012, when the nation was gripped with our own version of Armageddon. It seems the predictions were true, at least for New Zealand. There was a shortage of a breakfast food staple for many New Zealanders. Marmite was disappearing from supermarket shelves. Yes, this black yeasty spread which is just as polarising as it sounds, was at risk of being gone from our plates.

Needless to say, Marmite is one of the quintessential New Zealand foods. Trying Marmite is a rite of passage for every tourist, so make sure to do it at least once. I will warn you it's not for the faint of heart. This yeast spread is difficult to describe. You will either love it or hate it, it's that simple. Just make sure not to mention Vegemite, the Australian version.

Fortunately, a full Marmageddon was avoided, and Marmite returned to our shelves a few months after the shortage. It has remained ever since and long let it reign.

# 28. THE BEST UDON

Udon Works is yet another restaurant on Dominion Road that you shouldn't miss. Udon is the name of the game, and they've mastered it. It's often busy and waiting times can stretch for as long as an hour because it's a small restaurant. In short: booking is advisable.

One of my favourite things is the presentation of the noodles. They use beautiful oversize bowls and plates, making for an amazing presentation. While the udon is the focus, the sides and appetizers are not to be missed. I love the soft-boiled egg and the chicken tempura, they're a perfect addition to any of the udon.

One really unique thing is there are both warm and cold options. This makes for an exciting culinary adventure if you haven't had many udon dishes. If one of your party isn't too keen on noodles, there is a full menu of donburi.

# 29. MILK STACHE

I'm a huge fan of a good chewy cookie, the chewier, the better. Moustache Milk & Cookie Bar has long sated this craving. They've also saved me from baking and proceeding to eat an entire batch of my own!

Chewy cookies are their specialty, alongside over-the-top cookie cakes and thick cookie pies. You can order the pies and cakes online, but for the cookies, you'll have to head to the store. They have two locations in Auckland, and one in Christchurch.

Alongside cookies, they do amazing shakes. But I find these to be a deadly combination as you'll struggle to finish both. Instead, add a cup of milk to your order. Served in plain, chocolate, banana, and strawberry. The serving size is much smaller and the sweetness level is less than a shake, a perfect complement to your cookie or pie purchase.

# 30. ENJOY THE TROPICS EVERYDAY

Gardening and plants have been a lifelong hobby of mine. Ever since my parents put me to work in their garden helping clean up and pull weeds, it's planted a seed (pun intended). I try to incorporate plants into my life no matter where I am, even buying flowers when on vacation for an extra pop of greenery.

So it's no wonder that I'm including the Auckland Wintergardens on this list. Located inside the Auckland Domain, which is a sprawling park grounds right next to the city. The Wintergardens are two huge greenhouses that house a range of tropical and subtropical plants.

The first usually has a revolving selection of seasonal plants, alongside an impressive collection of cacti and succulents. With some of these being decades old. The second has a major focus on tropicals, and you'll be in awe of the travellers palm right as you walk in. It's easily 10m tall and nearly hitting the ceiling, truly crazy to see such a specimen indoors. There is an impressive collection of pitcher plants, begonias, syngoniums, aroids, and many more genera housed in the greenhouse.

Of course, there is a café within 100m of the Wintergardens. This is a cute little café that even has a high tea that you can book in advance. It's an easy spot to pop in before or after checking out the Wintergardens to rejuvenate.

# 31. MEAT & 3 VEGE: NEW ZEALAND TAKEAWAY STYLE

A classic takeout option in New Zealand is a roast. For the uninitiated, this is a classic meat and three veg situation. There's usually a choice of beef, lamb or pork. And for the veg, it's usually potatoes, kumara (sweet potato), pumpkin and some combination of peas, corn or carrots. Everything is smothered in gravy, and sometimes you'll get a bun, fried bread, or a Cornish pasty.

You'll see these shops dotted around the suburbs selling roasts. Often in close proximity to a fish and chips shop or a dairy (convenience store). I won't bother listing any that you should check out, because the best roast is a spur-of-the-moment decision.

Roasts are for when you're at the beach, the sun is setting and you're ready for a big meal after a day of exploring. Extremely portable, you can take these back down to the beach or head over to a park to enjoy. If you don't manage to stumble upon a roast shop during your time, Bird on a Wire does a delicious roast chicken with all the sides you could dream of.

# 32. IS THERE A NATIONAL DISH?

Fish and Chips could arguably be the national dish of New Zealand. Up and down the country there are hundreds of individually owned fish and chip shops, often run by families. They're all very similar and serve similar types of food. Battered fish and a scoop of chips are the classic combination. Add on a tin of tomato sauce or tartare sauce for the ultimate beach picnic.

The simpleness and portability is the main reason behind fish and chips popularity across the country. New Zealand is a very egalitarian country, and fish and chips being the national dish make perfect sense in this context. It's such a comfort food and so easy to bring to the beach, to the park, or to your best mate's house.

There are plenty of other options at most fish and chip shops. You'll find anything and everything deep fried. From the more obvious like hotdogs and hashbrowns to more exotic dishes like deep-fried bananas and Moro bars. The best bit is everything is usually very inexpensive. This is a time for exploration, so order your fish and chips, and then add anything else that catches your fancy.

If deep-fried isn't your thing, most places will have burgers and sometimes a variety of stir-fries. Be warned though that the star is the fish and chips, so these other options can be a bit hit or miss.

# 33. EDIBLE ART

Calling this next spot ice cream is a bit of an understatement and almost an insult. Giapo used to be on Queen St right by the theatre. And if you ever managed to get in without a line you'd consider yourself lucky. Now located towards the waterfront it's heavily refocused on experimental ice cream. You will never get a simple scoop on a cone here. Everything is an experience.

I wish I could give you some favourite flavours, but these change all the time and often sell out.

Sometimes you'll find cookies with ice cream, sometimes it's a taco ice cream, and sometimes they're baking up the best hot cross buns you'll have. It really is a place to experience. My one gripe is the portions can be overwhelming for one person. So it's best to either come in hungry or buy one to share.

# 34. TRANSPORT YOURSELF TO JAPAN

There are all sorts of hidden bars across Auckland, however, there are not that many hidden restaurants. While The Don isn't technically hidden, it has a fairly unassuming sign and is down a set of stairs on a busy street in central Auckland. So you'd be forgiven for walking right past where it is. Even I find myself missing the entryway, and I've been there a half dozen times!

What awaits you as you journey down the stairs, is a trip to Japan. The Don is very authentic and will make you feel as though you're in a restaurant in Tokyo. Once inside there is no outside world, there is only you, the menu and an incredibly cosy ambience. The tables are small, crammed together, and yet somehow the see-through bamboo blinds give you a sense of privacy.

The Don is known for yummy and inexpensive Japanese food. Their donburis are excellent, and they serve a wide range of typical Japanese dishes which are all equally good. A really neat thing is they are gluten-free friendly. They have separate GF soy sauce and mayonnaise, not something you can say about every Japanese restaurant.

# 35. CURRY GALORE

Have you ever watched an anime where they're eating curry, and it's the most beautiful thing? Japanese Dining You specialises in this fantastical Japanese curry. It's inexpensive and ridiculously filling. There are usually 2-3 options for curry, mild, medium, and a vegetarian option. These can all be paired with either rice or udon, and you can upsize to large for free. Yes, that's right, small and large portions cost the same. Don't ask me how they do it, I haven't got a clue!

A hot Japanese curry is a perfect meal when Auckland decides to be cold and rainy. Add on some tempura shrimp or mashed potatoes for the ultimate comfort food. You'll likely end up taking some of your meal with you as the portions are so huge. Which in my book is a good thing!

They also have a range of ramen and udon, but the curry is the real star of this restaurant. Japanese Dining You is definitely an insiders restaurant. It's somewhat hidden on the ground floor of a residential building on Hobson Street, and it has minimal signage. Even so, it's only a five min walk from Queen Street.

# 36. CAN'T DECIDE? GO TO THE STABLES

For times when you're in a group and just can't decide what to get, head over to one of the best food courts in Auckland. Elliott Stables is on Elliott Street, sitting just behind Smith & Caughey Department Store.

This is definitely more of an upmarket location, so expect prices to be a little higher than your average café. There are still deals to be had, with many of the restaurants having a lunchtime special. Have a walk around, then order and enjoy delicious food.

I'm a sucker for a good pizza or burger, so I usually go for one of these. The kumara fries at the burger joint are particularly good and honestly large enough for a light meal on their own.

# 37. PEANUT BUTTER NOODLES?

I'm far from an expert on noodles, but I've been told this is a somewhat unique take on Dan Dan Noodles. I'm talking about Basu Lounge in Takapuna of course. Their Dan Dan noodles aren't to be missed if you've ventured over the bridge to the North Shore.

The thick noodles look quite unassuming when you get them, but the sauce hidden on the bottom is the star. Mix up well and enjoy a flavour sensation. The peanut butter almost emulsifies with the stewed pork, then coats the noodles and creates a unique umami flavour. Get a large size and don't look back. You'll devour them faster than you thought possible, and then be left in the best food coma possible.

Lucky for you, Takapuna beach is right there for you to walk off your noodle baby. This happens to be one of the nicer beaches in Auckland, so take in the view while you're here. One of my favourite things to do is stop and use one of the two swings along the beachfront. They're incredibly sketchy, being tied to a couple of trees. But they're so much fun it's worth the risk!

# 38. VEGAN PORK BELLY?

Khu Khu is the premiere vegan restaurant in Auckland. Located on Ponsonby Road Khu Khu will make you rethink what vegan food is all about. The cuisine here is Thai, but everything has been made using vegan ingredients. It's easy to miss this though, with dishes like pork belly and fried chicken on the menu. What's great is it's not very expensive, firmly in the mid-tier without compromising on quality or portion size.

I won't lie to you and say it's a 100% dupe for meat, it's more like 85%. That doesn't mean the food isn't delicious though, and the meat substitutes are the best you'll find in Auckland. The sweet and sour fried chicken and pork belly stir fry are my favourites. Honestly, there aren't any bad choices here, be guided by your heart or ask for a recommendation.

The menu changes often, so if you're in Auckland for a while, be sure to check it out a few times. The cocktails and desserts deserve a special mention. The cocktails are light and refreshing and you'll feel like trying them all. The desserts change from time to time, but again are usually light and not too heavy, perfect after a big meal!

# 39. ISLAND GELATO COMPANY

New Zealand isn't short on excellent ice cream companies. The Island Gelato Company was founded on Waiheke Island and now has three outlets in the city. Amusingly one of them is on the pier where you can catch a boat to Waiheke. Meaning if you've visited Waiheke and already miss the ice cream, you're only 45-60 mins away from another scoop!

The flavours of Gelato are all fantastic and will leave you wanting more. From Espresso Martini to Sicilian Pistachio, to Gin, Grapefruit & Yuzu. They use fresh ingredients and are masters of making amazing Gelato. You can also order a Gelato cake, which in my opinion is the best type of cake!

# 40. THE BEST SANDWICHES IN DEDWOOD

Sandwiches are a staple meal for many New Zealanders. It's something we all grow up with eating at school for lunch. And many of us continue this tradition when we start working. A sandwich can be as simple as a few ingredients, or as over the top as what is on offer at Dedwood Deli.

A little-known fact is that Ponsonby was originally named Dedwood, and that's where the name originates. Of course, it's located on Ponsonby Road. Sandwiches have been taken to the next level. Many of the ingredients are made in-house, and the flavours really show this.

My favourites are the Chimichurri Steak and Pulled Brisket Roll. The waffle fries make for an ideal partner to these sandwiches. A fair warning that you'll struggle to finish everything in one sitting. The portions are massive and fortunately, the flavours are just as good cold as they are warm. Head in-store or order online for delivery, these sandwiches make a perfect hangover meal or for when you can't stand getting out of bed.

# 41. COFFEE IN A TUX

Anime boys in suits serving some of the city's best coffee? Need I explain further?

The Receptionist has two branches, both within five mins walk away. The one you want is on High Street, tucked down a short alley it's a little bit hidden. The baristas are in formal wear and look ridiculously dashing. They wouldn't be out of place at a Japanese host club. Except there's no funny business here. It's all about coffee and the team has spent a lot of time building up their reputation for quality brews.

My favourite and go-to order is an iced americano, perfect on a hot day in Auckland. And these guys do it like no one else. Order for takeaway or sit down and enjoy a croissant with your cup of coffee.

Amano Bakery that we covered earlier is around an 8-10min walk away, so you can also pick up some pastries from there and coffee from the Receptionist. Then sit in Chancery Square and people-watch while you enjoy yourself.

# 42. FARRO FRESH

When you're looking for something a bit more sophisticated, Farro is the supermarket of choice. With stores all over Auckland, it's a bit more than a deli but a bit less than a full-blown supermarket. Farro focuses more on specialty ingredients and boasts an impressive range of deli options and ready-made meals.

If you're just visiting you likely wouldn't ever head into a Farro. But if you're a foodie, it's a great way to experience the best of local food producers from all over the country. A perfect stop-off if you need to cater a picnic, Farro will have everything you require.

For a relatively inexpensive but very Parisian experience, Farro offers a rotisserie chicken deal, one chicken + 2 sides that you can choose from their deli. Add in some brioche buns and you can make your own roast chicken sliders! If they run out, you can also head to any supermarket and they also do rotisserie chickens. My favourite is the Waitoa free-range ones from Countdown. They seem to be extra juicy and fairly consistent between different stores.

# 43. THEY'LL GUT YOU LIKE A FISH!

New Zealand is well known for its bounty of seafood. What you might be surprised to learn is that seafood doesn't tend to be eaten often by most New Zealanders! The reason for this is a lot of our seafood ends up exported overseas, and what is left is often quite expensive compared to other meats. This is a bit sad, but let's not focus on that. Let's delve into the seafood we can get our hands on at the Auckland Fish Market!

Now I don't know about you, but I love to head to a market even if I don't buy anything. I love seeing what's on offer. I love checking the prices to compare to what we pay back home. And if I'm lucky there's something I can buy on the spot to try.

The Auckland Fish Market is part processing plant, part market, part food stall. Come early to view the wholesale auction, or later in the day to check out what is available to the public. There are heaps of places to get takeaways or a sit-down meal. One you cannot miss is the Lobster & Tap Lobster Roll. You get a healthy serving of lobster smothered in mayo and then slid into a warm bun, YUM!

# 44. NEW YORK, NEW YORK

There are many steak houses in Auckland, and my favourite is by far not the best. Tony's Steakhouse is the oldest running steakhouse in Auckland. It has an old-timey charm that I just can't resist. The recipes haven't changed much over the decades, and honestly, I can see why. If you've got a winning recipe, why change it?

The décor will make you think you've stepped into a New York restaurant. Its dark wooden panelling and dim lighting almost remind me of a cigar club. There are two specialties here – steak and pasta. Both are equally solid choices. The steaks are dry-aged, and after having tried almost every variation I can attest to their quality. The mushroom sauce steak with kumara mash and salad is my go-to order.

Will this be the best steak you've had? No. Will you feel like you've stepped back in time? Yes. Will the steak be great? Yes!

There's a great selection of traditional desserts as well, and they do fairly decent cocktails. I will say the wine menu leaves something to be desired. For a steak house, they don't really have any overly nice wines. So I prefer to skip the wine and just head straight into gin martinis.

# 45. DINE AT A HIDDEN FOOD COURT

Ponsonby is not a place where you'd expect to find a food court. It's a place where fashion and creatives intersect with excellent dining options for every taste. Nevertheless, there on Ponsonby Road at number 106 you will find the Ponsonby International Food Court.

Frequented by the office workers in the area, this food court isn't pretentious, it just serves damn tasty food. As the name suggests, you can find any type of cuisine at this food court. The meals are all delicious and filling at an attractive price point. If you're in the area and looking for a nice simple meal without all the fuss of a restaurant or café.

# 46. YOUR NEW FAVOURITE ICE CREAM SPOT

If you love the type of ice cream that is brave in its flavours, and generous with its additions, then Duck Island is perfect for you. Originally from Hamilton, Auckland has firmly embraced the delicious ice creams. With flavours like Salted Cacao Brownie, Chocolate Cherry Chunk, and White Chocolate Pomegranate, it's easy to see why.

There are two stores, one in Ponsonby and one in Newmarket. Both are extremely popular, and the Ponsonby store in particular often has a line out the door from 6 pm till closing. They bring in new flavours on a regular basis and are very good at catering to vegans with eight options at all times. Most flavours can be done gluten-free, and they keep these out at the back.

My favourite thing to order is the flight. This is a bowl with 8 mini scoops of ice cream. This is a perfect way to experience as many flavours as possible, and a perfect choice for 2-3 people. You can also buy some flavours in supermarkets if you can't make it to the store.

Being on Ponsonby Road, the Duck Island store makes a perfect way to round out dinner. When you're too full for a dessert, Duck Island sits in that ideal niche of not too large and not too small. For those that are super full, the tiddler is a perfect pick as it's a small scoop. And yes it's for kids, but who cares!

# 47. LA DOLCE VITA

It was a sad day in Auckland foodie history when the beloved Parnell French Market announced its closure. Fortunately, it's being resurrected with an Italian twist! Buono Delicatessen is officially taking over the lease from La Cigale. I know myself and all the foodies are frothing at our mouths waiting to return to this market.

While this is technically a market, the reality is there's more food to eat than anything else. Yes, you can get all your fresh fruits and veggies, breads, spreads, preserves, wines and more. But the draw card for most people is the huge range of food. Food trucks and producers from all over Auckland come together to create one of the best markets in Central Auckland. The best bit is that you can easily walk here from the CBD.

# 48. TAKE A TRIP DOWN HISTORY LANE

New Zealand is one of the youngest countries in the world, but it has a wealth of history to uncover. From pre-colonialism when Māori settled the country, through the colonial takeover, and up to modern days. New Zealand also has a rich biodiversity thanks to its isolation. Fortunately for you, both can be discovered in a single spot at the Auckland War Memorial Museum.

You might have sighted the neo-classical building while exploring Auckland, as it sits on top of a dormant volcano and overlooks the harbour. It's a stunning building just on its own, but even better is what is inside. Locals can get in for free, while visitors need to buy tickets. Although with so many migrants calling Auckland home, you can have a go at pretending to be a local and see how far you get!

The New Zealand history sections, and especially the ones on Māori culture are excellent. They're a great introduction to both colonial and Māori history if you can't make it to a more authentic Māori experience. Two attractions not to miss are the earthquake house and the volcanic eruption simulation video. Both are iconic and show the raw power sitting under the very land you're standing on.

Some of my favourite sections are the dinosaur exhibit and the dried specimens section. There's something so exciting about seeing how massive dinosaurs really were, and this museum is one of the few with a permanent exhibit. They used to have live insects, reptiles and amphibians, but these have recently been removed. You still have a huge selection of dried specimens to peruse and get to see some of the hardest-to-view fauna in New Zealand – insects.

# 49. FLAKY, SOFT, DELICIOUS

Uncle Mans is known all over the city for their handmade rotis. If you're lucky you'll catch them making them which is quite a spectacle. The way they handle the dough, flip it, and stretch it out before folding it to be cooked is quite fascinating to watch.

The highlights here are the Roti Canai with Chicken Curry or Beef Rendang. I am someone who can't handle their spice at all. But both dishes are worth powering through, and I have done so many a time. The beef is a bit spicier but not by a huge amount. Both are probably on the medium side of spicy.

Of course, there is a huge range of Malaysian dishes that are equally as delicious as the roti canai. Chicken Laksa and Tahu Sumbat are two of my favourites. There are a few different outlets of Uncle Mans, but the OG is on K'road, and this is the only one I'd go to.

# 50. GARDEN VILLAS

While not technically in Auckland, Hamilton is only a 1.5-hour drive. And when you consider half of that time is spent reaching the city limits of Auckland, you might understand why I feel safe including it. Plus this is one of the most magical gardens in all of New Zealand.

The Hamilton Botanical Gardens have made a name for themselves with one word: Villas.

They have created the most amazing villa gardens in completely different styles. You have the Chinese and Japanese villas, showcasing zen design and a great way to contrast these two cultures. There's an English cottage villa with all the beautiful wildflowers the UK is known for. I won't bore you with the rest, it's best to experience these in person, or check them out on google! The other villas are Italian, Indian, Modernist, Herb, Sustainable, Māori, Kitchen, Ancient Egyptian, Surrealist, Tudor, and Concept.

You can tell from the names these are going to be great, and once you see the scale of them in person you'll understand why I've included them in this book even though it's not in Auckland proper.

# OTHER RESOURCES:

https://at.govt.nz/

https://concreteplayground.com/auckland/

https://wikitravel.org/en/Auckland

https://www.aucklandisite.com/

https://www.aucklandnz.com/visit

https://www.eventfinda.co.nz/whatson/events/auckland

# READ OTHER BOOKS BY
# CZYK PUBLISHING

# Eat Like a Local

Follow *Eat Like a Local on* Amazon.
Join our mailing list for new books

http://bit.ly/EatLikeaLocalbooks


CZYKPublishing.com

Made in the USA
Monee, IL
11 April 2025

15569192R00046